T0059499

The
Go·and·Tell
STORYBOOK

30 *Bible Stories Showing*
Why We Share about Jesus

Laura Richie

Illustrated by Ian Dale

CHASING HOPE | PRESS

THE GO-AND-TELL STORYBOOK
Published by David C Cook
4050 Lee Vance Drive
Colorado Springs, CO 80918 U.S.A.

Integrity Music Limited, a Division of David C Cook
Brighton, East Sussex BN1 2RE, England

The graphic circle C logo is a registered trademark of David C Cook.

Library of Congress Control Number 2022930418
ISBN 978-0-8307-8295-6
eISBN 978-0-8307-8296-3

Text © 2022 Laura Richie
Illustrations © 2022 Ian Dale

The Team: Laura Derico, Stephanie Bennett, Judy Gillispie, James Hershberger
Design and Illustration: Ian Dale

Printed in India
First Edition 2022

1 2 3 4 5 6 7 8 9 10

032822

To Josiah, Grace, Isaiah, Elisha,
and
Perry "PaPa" Wimpey, whose generosity and hospitality
remind me of some in this book.
—Laura

To Eva and Ezra,
may God fill your lives
with stories to tell.
—Ian

The Bible Storybook Series

The Advent Storybook
The Easter Storybook
The Go-and-Tell Storybook

BOARD BOOKS
Count My Way to Jesus
Just Like Jesus
My First Advent Storybook
My First Easter Storybook

COLORING BOOK
The Advent Storybook Coloring Book

FROM THE AUTHOR

Dear Reader,

I often forget that my life is part of a bigger story that stretches back to the dawn of Creation. The joys and trials, blessings and tears that fill my days are connected to a larger whole—not only to the people around me and the God who made me, but also to the lives of people long gone and those yet to come. It's like a mosaic—each life a tiny tile carefully placed with the others to create something beautiful. God is the artist who skillfully arranges chipped pieces, bringing life and beauty and goodness.

The apostle Paul, whom you will meet in this book, described this connection as a body. Those who believe that Jesus is the Rescuer become a part of Jesus' body—they join Him in the good that He's doing and share in His life. Each part of the body has a special job, but all parts work together. If one of our body parts is sick, our whole body hurts and needs healing.

I like this word picture the most because I'm a nurse.

Sickness and disease are some of the many sad, broken things in our world. I'm so glad that Jesus is working to end evil, sickness, and death. He's working to make all things new!

The Go-and-Tell Storybook continues the story first told in *The Advent Storybook* and then in *The Easter Storybook*. Jesus the King is bringing His good kingdom. We'll see that Jesus' work of making all things new and good didn't end when He returned to His Father. Instead, God's Spirit came and continued the rescue. God came to be with His people, drawing them close to Himself and to each other. Because of God's Spirit, our lives have a purpose—we each have a unique role to play in going and telling and living out this story of rescue and hope!

May we join Jesus in His work and also rest in His grace.

Blessings,

Laura Richie

The Promise of God's Spirit
An Introduction

Long ago, when the world was new, people walked and talked with God. They loved God, and they loved each other. God gave them a beautiful garden as their home, and everything was very good.

But an evil serpent whispered lies, and when people believed those lies, everything shattered. Death and pain entered the world—and all seemed lost. But God spoke a promise: one day a Son would come to crush evil forever.

Through the centuries, people waited, longing for the Promised Son.

Then, in the fullness of time, He came! Once again, people walked and talked with God. Jesus came to remind people of God's love and to help *them* love. He died in our place, then came back to life to fix our broken friendships with God, with each other, and with all creation. When it was time, Jesus returned to His Father, but He didn't leave His friends alone.

Jesus spoke a promise: one day soon, God's Spirit would come and continue His work of making all things good and new again.

Jesus' friends waited, hoping once again to walk and talk with God.

And then He came.

You shall know that I am in the midst of Israel,
  and that I am the Lord your God and there
    is none else.
And my people shall never again be put to shame.

And it shall come to pass afterward,
  that I will pour out my Spirit on all flesh;
your sons and your daughters shall prophesy,
  your old men shall dream dreams,
  and your young men shall see visions.
Even on the male and female servants
  in those days I will pour out my Spirit.

And I will show wonders in the heavens and on the earth, blood and fire and columns of smoke. The sun shall be turned to darkness, and the moon to blood, before the great and awesome day of the Lord comes. And it shall come to pass that everyone who calls on the name of the Lord shall be saved.

JOEL 2:27–32a

The wilderness and the dry land shall be glad;
    the desert shall rejoice and blossom like the crocus;
it shall blossom abundantly
    and rejoice with joy and singing.
The glory of Lebanon shall be given to it,
    the majesty of Carmel and Sharon.
They shall see the glory of the Lord,
    the majesty of our God.

Strengthen the weak hands,
    and make firm the feeble knees.
Say to those who have an anxious heart,
    "Be strong; fear not!
Behold, your God
    will come with vengeance,
with the recompense of God.
    He will come and save you."

Then the eyes of the blind shall be opened,
    and the ears of the deaf unstopped;
then shall the lame man leap like a deer,
    and the tongue of the mute sing for joy.

For waters break forth in the wilderness,
    and streams in the desert;
the burning sand shall become a pool,
    and the thirsty ground springs of water;
in the haunt of jackals, where they lie down,
    the grass shall become reeds and rushes.

And a highway shall be there,
    and it shall be called the Way of Holiness;
the unclean shall not pass over it.
    It shall belong to those who walk on the way;
    even if they are fools, they shall not go astray.
No lion shall be there,
    nor shall any ravenous beast come up on it;
they shall not be found there,
    but the redeemed shall walk there.
And the ransomed of the LORD shall return
    and come to Zion with singing;
everlasting joy shall be upon their heads;
    they shall obtain gladness and joy,
    and sorrow and sighing shall flee away.

ISAIAH 35:1–10

MAP 1

Jerusalem

Known as the holy city and the city of God, among other names, Jerusalem is a special place for followers of Jesus. Jesus came there first as a baby, taught in the Temple as a child, and then many years later died and rose again in this city. Jesus' disciples first received God's Spirit in Jerusalem, and then they went out from this place to go and tell the world the good news about Jesus Christ, the Messiah, our Rescuer. As you read the stories of the first Christians, look for some of the places they went.

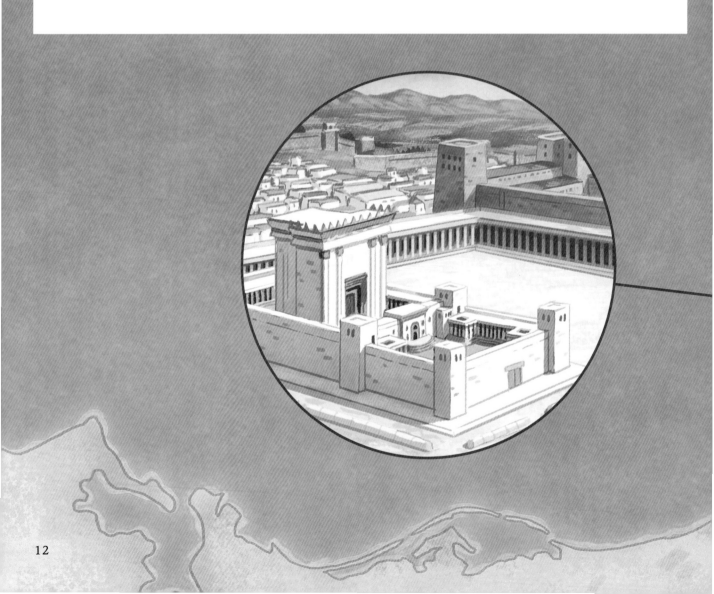

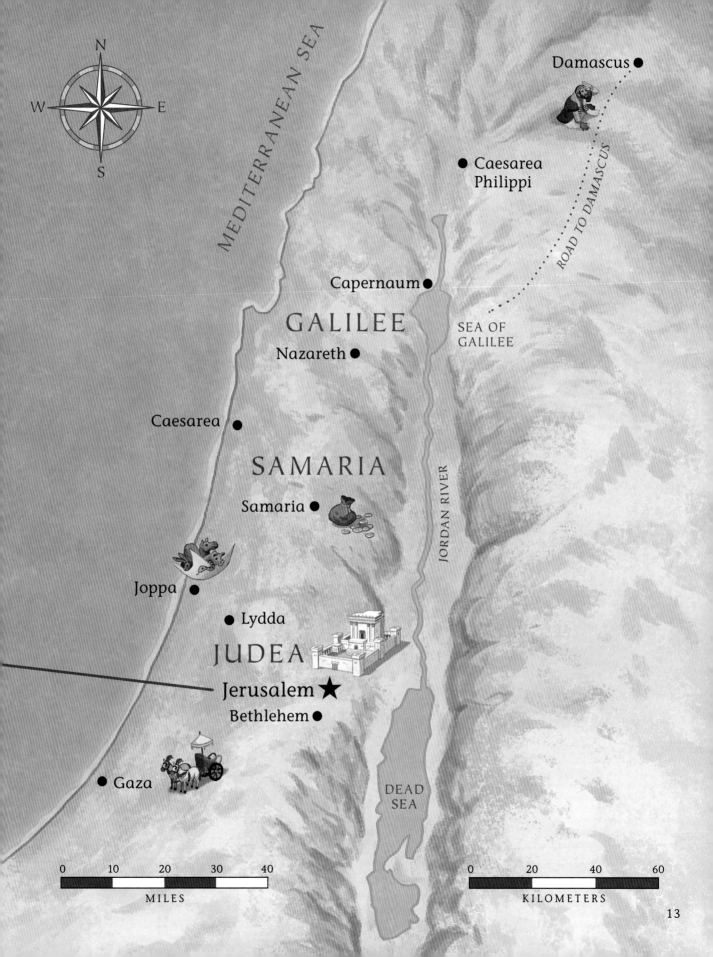

N
W · E
S

MEDITERRANEAN SEA

Damascus ●

● Caesarea
Philippi

ROAD TO DAMASCUS

Capernaum ●

GALILEE

SEA OF
GALILEE

Nazareth ●

Caesarea ●

SAMARIA

Samaria ●

JORDAN RIVER

Joppa ●

● Lydda

JUDEA

Jerusalem ★

Bethlehem ●

DEAD
SEA

● Gaza

0   10   20   30   40
MILES

0   20   40   60
KILOMETERS

13

God's Spirit Comes
Acts 1–2

"Turn to me and be saved, all the ends of the earth! For I am God, and there is no other."
ISAIAH 45:22

Jesus' friends waited. Not long ago they watched Jesus rise up in the sky with a cloud. Before He left, He spoke a promise: "You will receive power when the Holy Spirit has come upon you, and you will be my witnesses in Jerusalem and in all Judea and Samaria, and to the end of the earth" (Acts 1:8). Being "witnesses" meant telling others about the Rescuer they had seen and His good kingdom.

Now it was Pentecost, when Jewish people celebrated God's goodness. Jesus' friends gathered to remember their Rescuer. They wondered when the Holy Spirit would come.

Then, as they waited, it happened.

Suddenly a loud sound—like a mighty rushing wind—came down from heaven and filled the whole house. Small flames spread out and rested on each person. Jesus' friends were all filled with God's Spirit! And the Spirit helped them speak in other languages.

Many Jewish families had traveled from other countries to Jerusalem to celebrate Pentecost. They heard the loud noise. Then they heard Jesus' friends telling the good things God had done. Everyone was amazed. "We hear them in our *own* languages!"

Jesus' friend Peter stood and explained: "Men of Israel, Jesus was sent from God, but you crucified Him, hanging Him on the cross. God raised Him back to life—He is stronger than death. We saw Jesus alive, and now He is with God, reigning as King. Jesus promised to send God's Spirit to be with us, and that's what you heard. Jesus is Lord and Christ!"

God's Spirit spoke to the people's hearts. They believed! They knew Jesus was the Son promised long ago. They needed to be rescued by Him. They asked, "What should we do?"

Peter answered, "Turn from your sins and be baptized in Jesus' name. God will forgive your sins and will send His Spirit to you. This promise is for you and for all who are far off."

And many of the Jewish people listening—about three thousand—believed and came close to God again! When they returned to their homes, they told others about Jesus.

. . . .

Who did Jesus send to the people who believed in Him?

He Walks!

Acts 3–4

Then shall the lame man leap like a deer, and the tongue of the mute sing for joy.
For waters break forth in the wilderness, and streams in the desert.
ISAIAH 35:6

Once there was a man who couldn't walk. Since his legs didn't work, he couldn't grow his own food or earn money at that time. Every day, his friends carried him to the Temple in Jerusalem. He sat outside and asked others for money and help.

One afternoon the man who couldn't walk saw two of Jesus' friends, Peter and John. He asked them for money. Peter said, "I have no silver and gold, but what I do have I give to you. In the name of Jesus Christ of Nazareth, rise up and walk!" (Acts 3:6).

What do you think happened next?

Peter grabbed the man's hand and pulled him to his feet. The man who had *never* walked stood right up! He was so excited that he jumped into the air! He leaped and praised God for making his broken legs good and new again.

All the people were amazed. They had seen that man begging by the Beautiful Gate for years.

Peter explained to everyone what had happened: "Faith in Jesus' name has made this man you know strong." Peter wanted everyone to believe that Jesus was the Rescuer.

Peter also said, "Turn away from your sins so that they may be blotted out and you may be with God and be refreshed. Jesus is the Messiah, God's Rescuer, and one day He will come back and restore all things, making them new and good again."

Many people who saw the man walk and heard Peter's words believed. But not *everyone* believed. The religious leaders were angry with Peter and told him to stop talking about Jesus and healing people. But Peter said, "There is salvation in no one else, for there is no other name under heaven given among men by which we must be saved" (4:12).

Peter knew Jesus was the Rescuer. The man whose legs were healed knew it too. God's Spirit helped Peter do the same good things that Jesus had done.

. . . .

What does it mean to have faith in Jesus? It means believing Jesus is the living Son of God who makes all things new.

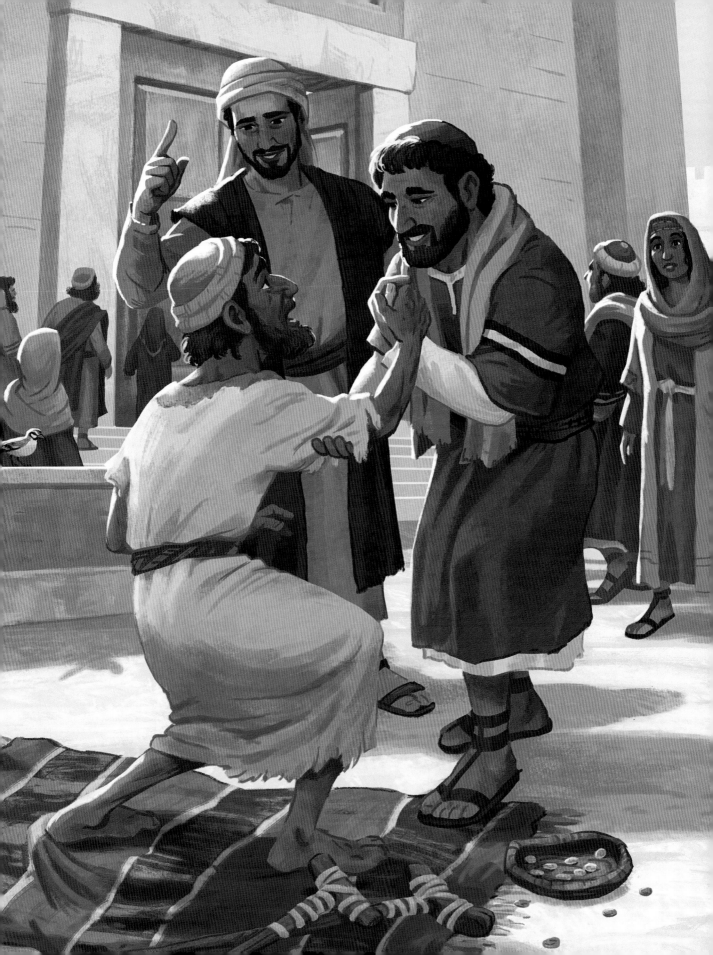

Go and Share
Acts 4–5

"I do not ask for these only, but also for those who will believe in me through their word, that they may all be one, just as you, Father, are in me, and I in you, that they also may be in us, so that the world may believe that you have sent me."
JOHN 17:20-21

God's Spirit moved among Peter and the rest of Jesus' friends, and He helped them love each other. They shared their food and money. They cared about others, not just themselves. Because they loved each other, no one was hungry. "Now the full number of those who believed were of one heart and soul.... There was not a needy person among them, for as many as were owners of lands or houses sold them and brought the proceeds of what was sold and laid it at the apostles' feet, and it was distributed to each as any had need" (Acts 4:32, 34–35).

A man named Barnabas (BAR-nuh-bus) sold a field and gave the money to some of Jesus' friends. Barnabas wanted to help other believers who needed food or clothes. Barnabas loved them.

But others just *pretended* to love people. Ananias (ANN-uh-NYE-us) and his wife, Sapphira (Suh-FYE-ruh), sold a field. They brought *some* of the money to Peter, but they kept part of it and lied about it. God's Spirit helped Peter know their secret. When Ananias realized Peter knew, he fell down and died. Then Sapphira died in the same way.

True friends do not lie. Jesus died and came back to life to give *us* life. He helps us live as true friends with God and each other.

God's Spirit continued to make things new and good again. People carried sick friends or family into the streets so Peter's shadow might fall on them as he walked by. Those who were sick or full of evil spirits came to Jesus' friends, and God's Spirit healed them all! Many people believed that Jesus was the Rescuer. They wanted to live in Jesus' kingdom of love.

. . . .

What does it mean to love? Love is wanting good for someone and then doing that good. Love is meeting the needs of others even when it is very hard to do. How would life be different if everyone loved like Barnabas and the other believers?

Go and Tell
Acts 5

In the beginning was the Word, and the Word was with God, and the Word was God.... In him was life, and the life was the light of men.
JOHN 1:1, 4

Jesus' good friends, also known as the apostles, told everyone about the Rescuer who came to make all things new. Many people were healed, and many believed. But the same religious leaders who hated Jesus now hated His friends. They wanted to get rid of the men who wouldn't stop talking about Jesus.

The leaders put the apostles in prison in Jerusalem. But God had a different plan. An angel of God opened the prison doors at night, set the apostles free, and said, "Go and stand in the temple and speak to the people all the words of this Life" (Acts 5:20).

So Jesus' friends escaped … then walked right back to the Temple to teach!

The religious leaders gathered for the trial the next day and asked for the prisoners. But when the guards opened the doors, the prison was empty! Then someone said, "Look! The men are back at the Temple teaching the people."

So the guards arrested Jesus' friends *again* and brought them to the leaders. The high priest said, "We told you not to speak about that man, yet you have filled the city with your teaching. You want us to be punished for His death."

Peter and the apostles answered, "We must obey God rather than men. You killed Jesus, but the one true God raised Him back to life. God placed Jesus at His right hand as Rescuer and King. Jesus forgives sins and brings us close to God and each other again. We saw these things, and so did God's Spirit, who is with us."

The chief priests were furious. They wanted to kill Jesus' friends. But a respected leader named Gamaliel (Guh-MAY-lee-el) spoke up. "Men of Israel, be careful. Leave these men alone. If they follow their own plans, they will fail, just like so many others. But if they are following God, *you* will fail. And you might find yourselves fighting against God!"

The leaders listened to Gamaliel, but they beat Jesus' friends before letting them go. Then every day and everywhere, the apostles told people about the Rescuer, Jesus.

. . . .

What did the angel tell the men to do? How does telling about Jesus help people?

20

Stephen Sees Jesus
Acts 6–7

And we all, with unveiled face, beholding the glory of the Lord, are being transformed into the same image from one degree of glory to another. For this comes from the Lord who is the Spirit.
2 CORINTHIANS 3:18

At that time, many people were coming close to God and each other. Even Jewish priests who worked in the Temple believed that Jesus was the chosen Rescuer. The apostles asked for helpers to serve all the new believers. A faithful man named Stephen, filled with God's Spirit, was chosen to be a helper. Stephen showed many people God's love and power.

But some people didn't like what Stephen was doing. A group of Jewish men told lies about Stephen, and he was arrested. The religious leaders asked Stephen if he really was saying false things about God and His laws and about Moses. As they waited for his answer, they noticed that Stephen's face shone with glory like an angel!

Stephen told them how God had planned from the beginning to rescue people. God had made a friendship promise with Abraham, and again with Moses. God rescued His people again and again, but they forgot about Him and His love. God led His people in the wilderness, but they still did evil. Then, when Jesus came to live among God's people, they killed the Promised Son.

Stephen said, "You and those before you have always worked against the Holy Spirit. You killed the prophets who spoke of the coming of the Messiah, whom you also betrayed and killed." Stephen spoke the truth, but this made the leaders very angry.

Then Stephen looked up into heaven and saw the glory of God. Stephen said, "Behold, I see the heavens opened, and the Son of Man standing at the right hand of God" (verse 56). Stephen saw Jesus! But the leaders didn't want to hear anything else. They all gave their cloaks to a young man named Saul to hold, and they picked up heavy stones to throw at Stephen.

Before he died, Stephen said, "Lord, do not hold this sin against them" (verse 60). God helped Stephen love these men, just as Jesus loved those who hurt and killed Him. And Stephen went to be with Jesus forever.

. . . .

Why did Stephen keep talking about Jesus even though it made some people angry?

Simon's Bad Magic
Acts 8

"Love your enemies and pray for those who persecute you, so that you may be sons of your Father who is in heaven. For he makes his sun rise on the evil and on the good."
MATTHEW 5:44–45a

Many followers of Jesus were mistreated by angry religious leaders in Jerusalem, so these followers left. And everywhere they went, they told people about Jesus. Philip, a Jewish friend of Stephen, went to Samaria. Most Jews *hated* Samaritans—they considered them "unclean" by their religious rules. But Philip knew that Jesus came to rescue *all* people, so he went to tell the Samaritans about Jesus.

The Samaritan crowds heard Philip's teaching and saw God's healing. Evil spirits came out of people, and many who couldn't walk were able to walk again. God's Spirit was making things good and new again! Many Samaritans believed that Jesus was the Messiah, God's Rescuer. They wanted to follow Jesus and live in God's good kingdom.

A Samaritan named Simon saw the miracles God was doing through Philip and was amazed! He believed that Jesus was the Rescuer too. Simon was a magician—he used magic to make people think he was strong and powerful. But his magic powers came from evil Satan, not God.

Now Jesus' friends Peter and John heard that many Samaritans had decided to follow Jesus. They traveled to Samaria and laid their hands on the new believers and prayed. God's Spirit came to be with the Samaritans in a way that everyone could see.

Simon saw how God's Spirit came through the disciples and wanted to have this same power for himself. Simon offered money to Jesus' friends and said, "Give me this power. I want to be able to lay my hands on people and give them the Holy Spirit."

But Peter saw Simon's greedy heart and said, "You can't buy the gift of God with money! Repent, because your heart is not right before God." Simon asked Peter to pray for him. He still had a lot to learn about God's goodness and grace.

God loves and rescues people as a gift. We can't do anything to earn His love. God brings us close to Himself and each other. He helps us love as He loves.

. . . .

Why did Philip, Peter, and John go to their enemies in Samaria?

The Ethiopian Believes
Acts 8

For thus says the LORD: "To the eunuchs who keep my Sabbaths, who choose the things that please me and hold fast my covenant, I will give in my house and within my walls a monument and a name better than sons and daughters."
ISAIAH 56:4–5a

After Philip told his new friends in Samaria about Jesus, an angel told Philip to go to a road in the middle of the desert! It didn't make sense, but Philip obeyed. When he arrived, Philip saw an important man riding in a chariot. God's Spirit told Philip, "Go over to the chariot." Men like Philip at this time almost never ran, but when Philip heard the Lord's command, he wasted no time. He ran right over to the stranger.

The rich man was from far away—he was a court official of the queen of Ethiopia, in a land we call Africa. He had learned about the one true God and had traveled all the way to Jerusalem to worship Him. Now the man was reading out loud from a scroll of God's prophet Isaiah. Philip asked if he understood the words. The man said, "How can I, unless someone guides me?" (Acts 8:31). And he invited Philip to sit with him.

The prophet's words were about Jesus: "Like a sheep he was led to the slaughter and like a lamb before its shearer is silent, so he opens not his mouth" (verse 32).

Philip explained that Jesus was the Promised Son of God. He died as a sacrifice, like a lamb offered to God, because of our sin. Then He came back to life to rescue us! Jesus came to bring us close again to God and each other. He made us a family.

The Ethiopian official didn't have a family of his own or children to carry on his name. But God would give him a family and remember his name. The man believed the good news about Jesus. He saw some water along the road and asked to be baptized right then. So Philip baptized him, welcoming him into God's family. The man's sins were washed away because of Jesus, the Rescuer. When they came up out of the water, God's Spirit carried Philip away. The queen's official didn't see Philip again, but he went on his way rejoicing. He would tell his friends at home about Jesus and how He was fixing broken friendships and this broken world.

. . . .

Why is it good to tell people who may live far away from us about Jesus? How does God's Spirit help people from every nation understand the good news about Jesus?

Saul and the Blinding Light
Acts 9

And a highway shall be there, and it shall be called the Way of Holiness; the unclean shall not pass over it ... but the redeemed shall walk there. And the ransomed of the LORD shall return and come to Zion with singing; everlasting joy shall be upon their heads.
ISAIAH 35:8–10a

Saul tried very hard to be good enough for God. He was a Pharisee—an expert in Jewish law. He didn't think Jesus was the Messiah, God's chosen Rescuer. Saul wanted everyone who followed Jesus as the Messiah to be punished. He thought these Jesus followers were dishonoring God. He mistreated all of Jesus' friends, both men and women—all who belonged to the Way, which was how the first Christians were described.

As Saul was on the road to Damascus to arrest more Jesus followers, suddenly a blinding light from heaven shone around him. Saul fell to the ground. He couldn't see anything! Then he heard a voice say, "Saul, Saul, why are you persecuting me?" (Acts 9:4).

Saul asked, "Who are you, Lord?"

The voice answered, "I am Jesus, whom you are persecuting. But rise and enter the city, and you will be told what you are to do" (verses 5–6). *Persecuting* means treating people badly because of their beliefs.

The men traveling with Saul helped him get to Damascus because he still couldn't see. Saul was blind and didn't eat or drink for three days—he just prayed.

A believer named Ananias lived in Damascus. God spoke to him in a vision, telling him where to find Saul. God told Ananias that Saul was waiting for him to lay hands on him so he could see again. Ananias was afraid. He knew the evil Saul had done to Jesus' friends. But God said, "Go on, for I will use Saul to tell about Me to Jews and non-Jews and even to kings." And God said that Saul would suffer for the sake of Jesus' name.

Ananias obeyed. He laid his hands on Saul and said, "Brother Saul, Jesus sent me so you may see again and be filled with the Holy Spirit." Immediately something like scales fell from Saul's eyes, and he could see! He was baptized, ate some food, and felt stronger.

Jesus changed Saul on that road to Damascus, and Saul walked with God's Spirit.

. . . .

How did God use Saul's blindness to help Saul see the truth about Jesus and His friends?

Aeneas and Tabitha
Acts 9

"Truly, truly, I say to you, whoever believes in me will also do the works that I do; and greater works than these will he do, because I am going to the Father."
JOHN 14:12

Saul began telling the Jews that Jesus was the Messiah. Everyone was amazed! The man who had once hated Jesus was now Jesus' friend. But the Jews who didn't believe in Jesus were very angry. They wanted to get rid of Saul. Saul's friends hid him in a big basket. Then they lowered him down the wall outside Damascus, and he escaped.

He went to Jerusalem, but Jesus' close friends didn't trust Saul at first. Peter and the other apostles knew the evil Saul had done. But Barnabas told them Saul had changed, so they decided to trust Saul. Then Saul told many people in Jerusalem that Jesus was the Messiah. Many believed and followed God, but some did not. They plotted to get rid of Saul. But Jesus' friends heard about their plan and sent Saul away to keep him safe.

Though Saul was having trouble, God's Spirit was building up the church. He was doing good things through Jesus' friend Peter as well. In a place called Lydda (LID-duh), Peter met Aeneas (uh-NEE-us), a man who hadn't been able to walk for eight years. Peter said, "Aeneas, Jesus Christ heals you; rise and make your bed" (Acts 9:34). And Aeneas was healed! People saw Aeneas walking around, and they believed that Jesus was the Rescuer.

In the nearby city of Joppa (JOP-puh), a kind woman named Tabitha died. She had helped many people, especially poor widows, and they were very sad that she was gone. Jesus' friends heard that Peter was close and sent for him. Peter went to Joppa right away. He found Tabitha's room filled with people weeping for her. Peter sent them all outside, knelt down, and prayed. Then he turned to her body and said, "Tabitha, arise" (verse 40).

And she did! Tabitha came back to life. She opened her eyes and sat up. Peter showed her friends that she was alive, and they were so happy. Many people believed in Jesus in that city too. God's Spirit was doing good things. And He wasn't finished yet!

. . . .

Who did Peter say was healing Aeneas? How do you think Tabitha's friends felt when God brought her back to life?

Cornelius's Full House
Acts 10

"Do you not see that whatever goes into the mouth passes into the stomach and is expelled? But what comes out of the mouth proceeds from the heart, and this defiles a person."
MATTHEW 15:17–18

Cornelius was a Roman soldier. He wasn't Jewish, but someone had told him about the one true God. One afternoon, God gave Cornelius a vision. In the vision, an angel came and said, "Cornelius, God has noticed your prayers and your gifts to help others. Send men to the city of Joppa to bring Simon Peter." And Cornelius obeyed.

The next day in Joppa, Peter went up on the flat roof to pray. He felt hungry. As he waited for lunch, he saw a vision: a large sheet, filled with animals, came down from the heavens. Many of the animals were called "unclean" by Jewish law. But a voice said, "Get up, Peter; kill and eat."

Peter was hungry, but he wasn't *that* hungry! As a Jewish man, he knew he couldn't eat unclean animals. So Peter answered, "By no means, Lord; for I have never eaten anything that is common or unclean" (Acts 10:14). But the voice said to Peter, "What God has made clean, do not call common" (verse 15).

This happened three times. Peter was confused and wondered what the vision meant. Right then, the men sent from Cornelius arrived. God's Spirit said to Peter, "Three men are looking for you. Go with them, because I have sent them." So Peter obeyed.

The next day Peter and some friends traveled with the men to Cornelius's house. Now, Jews weren't supposed to go into the "unclean" houses of Gentiles, or non-Jews. And Cornelius's house was full of his family and friends, waiting to hear Peter's words.

Then Peter remembered the vision from God. He said, "I understand now that God accepts anyone, even those from other nations, who honor Him and do what is right." Peter told them about Jesus, the Rescuer, who died and came back to life to make all things new. Peter said, "Everyone who believes in Jesus receives forgiveness of sins through His name."

Cornelius and the people in his house believed! God's Spirit came to be with them, even though they were Gentiles. Jesus came to rescue *all* who believe, both Jews and Gentiles.

. . . .

What did Peter learn about "unclean" things? Are there any people God doesn't want us to tell about Jesus?

Rome

ADRIATIC
SEA

MACEDONIA

ITALY

Philippi

Thessalonica

Berea

AEGEAN
SEA

ACHAIA

SICILIA

Corinth   Athens

Syracuse

MALTA

MAP

2

Paul's Travels

Paul became a bold preacher, and he traveled to many places to tell as many people as he could about Jesus. When he was known as Saul, an expert in Jewish law, he was sure that every Jewish person should obey only God's law. Now Paul had a new heart filled with God's Spirit. He believed that Jesus was the Promised Son of God, and Paul was sure that every person should know the gift of God's grace. As you hear the stories of Paul's travels, look on the map to see where he went, teaching everyone about Jesus, the Rescuer.

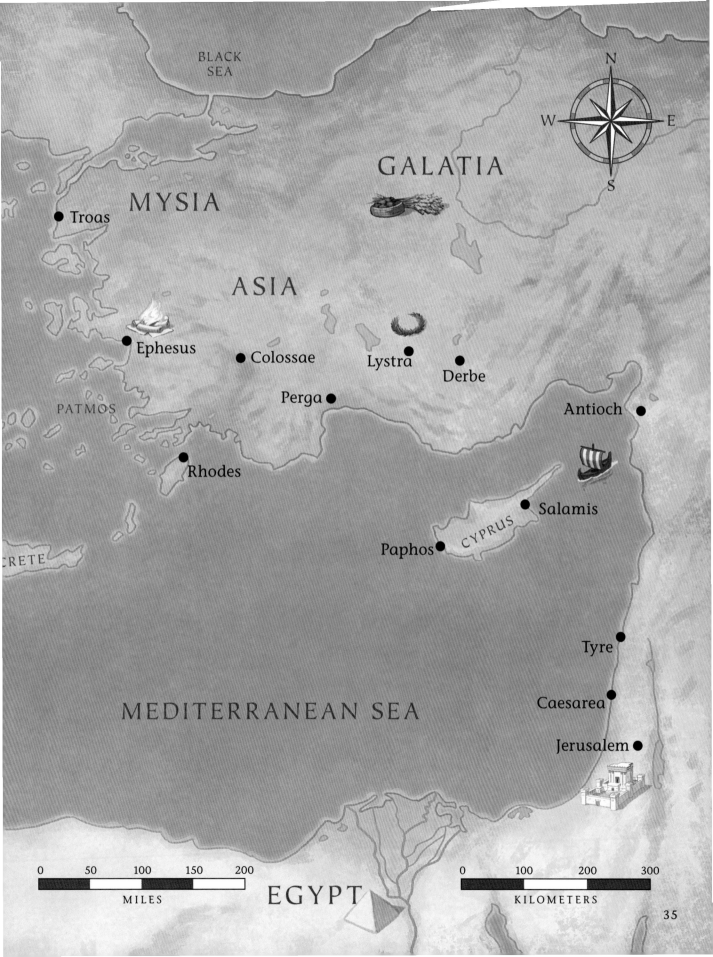

BLACK
SEA

GALATIA

MYSIA

Troas

ASIA

Ephesus

Colossae

Lystra

Derbe

PATMOS

Perga

Antioch

Rhodes

Salamis

CYPRUS

CRETE

Paphos

MEDITERRANEAN SEA

Tyre

Caesarea

Jerusalem

| 0 | 50 | 100 | 150 | 200 |

MILES

| 0 | 100 | 200 | 300 |

EGYPT

KILOMETERS

35

Amazing Escape
Acts 12

"For truly, I say to you, if you have faith like a grain of mustard seed, you will say to this mountain, 'Move from here to there,' and it will move, and nothing will be impossible for you."
MATTHEW 17:20

God's Spirit was doing many good things, but some Jewish people didn't like that. Those who didn't believe were angry. They thought Jesus was just a pretend Messiah. And some of the Jews who *did* believe were also upset. They didn't want their enemies from other nations to believe and be rescued. Peter, Saul, Barnabas, and the others kept telling more people that Jesus was the Rescuer, but this mission was often difficult for them.

Then a very sad thing happened. One of Jesus' close friends named James was killed by King Herod. James's death pleased some of the Jews, so Herod arrested Peter too. But the Jews who believed in Jesus were very scared for Peter, and they prayed hard for him.

That night, Peter was sleeping between two soldiers. He was chained to each soldier, and other soldiers guarded the door—there was no way Peter could escape.

Suddenly a bright light filled the dark prison. An angel woke Peter and said, "Get up!" The chains fell off Peter's hands. The angel said, "Get dressed." So Peter did. Then the angel said, "Wrap up in your cloak and follow me." The angel took Peter past two guards to an iron gate. The gate opened by itself, and they walked along the street. Once Peter was free, the angel disappeared.

When Peter realized that God really had rescued him, he went to Mary's house. Many people were gathered inside, praying for him. Peter knocked at the door, and a servant named Rhoda came to answer. When Rhoda heard Peter's voice, she ran back to tell everyone that Peter was out of prison. She was so excited that she forgot to let Peter inside!

Peter kept knocking, and Rhoda kept telling everyone it was Peter. No one believed her, but when they opened the door, it really was Peter. God had rescued him!

Everyone was so amazed to see that Peter had been set free. Peter explained how the angel had rescued him. And they remembered that with God all things are possible.

. . . .

Have you ever seen God do something that seemed impossible? What is something you would like to see God do?

Elymas in the Mist
Acts 13

"I will make you as a light for the nations, that my salvation may reach to the end of the earth."
ISAIAH 49:6b

One day Saul, also called Paul, was worshipping God in the city of Antioch. While the believers fasted and prayed, God's Spirit said, "Set apart Barnabas and Saul for God's work." So the believers laid hands on Barnabas and Saul and sent them off. Paul and Barnabas sailed to the island of Cyprus—where Barnabas had grown up. Together with a helper called John Mark, they told people all over the island that Jesus was the Rescuer.

When they had almost reached the other end of the island, they met a pretend Jewish prophet named Elymas (el-OO-mahs). He was a magician who did magic by Satan's evil power. Elymas worked for the most important leader on the island, the proconsul. Elymas didn't want the important leader to know God, so he told the leader lies.

Paul was filled with God's Spirit and knew what was happening. He told Elymas, "Stop making the straight paths of the Lord out to be crooked. Now God's hand is on you, and you will be blind for a time." Mist and darkness came on Elymas right then, and he couldn't see. But the proconsul saw God's power. He believed Paul's words about Jesus.

Paul and Barnabas sailed to other cities, telling everyone about Jesus. In one city, Paul stood up in the Jewish church, called a synagogue. He told people about the Messiah promised long ago. He said, "Through Jesus, the Savior, your sins can be forgiven. Everyone who believes can be free. The law of Moses could never set us free, but Jesus can."

The Jewish people begged Paul to tell them more about Jesus. On the Sabbath, the day set aside for God, the whole city gathered to hear Paul. The religious leaders were jealous. They didn't want "unclean" Gentiles to hear about the Rescuer. But Paul and Barnabas told the truth—Jesus came to rescue *all* people. When the Gentiles heard this message, they were so happy! Many believed and were filled with God's Spirit. But those who didn't believe were angry. They forced Paul and Barnabas to leave.

. . . .

Why did Elymas want to keep the proconsul, a leader with a lot of power, from believing in Jesus?

Crowds in Lystra
Acts 14

"Behold, at that time I will deal with all your oppressors. And I will save the lame and gather the outcast, and I will change their shame into praise and renown in all the earth."
ZEPHANIAH 3:19

Paul and Barnabas came to a city called Lystra (LISS-truh). Crowds gathered to hear Paul speak. In the crowd was a man who had never walked. His feet had been broken since he was born. He listened as Paul talked about Jesus, the Rescuer.

Paul could tell the man believed. He said loudly to the man, "Stand up on your feet."

And he jumped up! The man who had never taken a step in his life started walking around! Everyone was amazed.

But the people in Lystra believed in many pretend gods. They thought that Barnabas and Paul were like their pretend gods Zeus and Hermes. The priest who lived at the temple of Zeus wanted to worship Paul and Barnabas with offerings of oxen and wreaths. But Paul and Barnabas tore their clothes in distress and rushed into the crowd.

They told everyone, "We are men just like you! We bring you good news so that you can turn from these pretend gods to a living God, who made the whole world and everything in it. He is the good God who gives you rain from heaven and food to eat."

The people still wanted to worship Paul and Barnabas. They were afraid their gods would punish them if they didn't. Then angry Jewish men from other cities came and stirred up the crowds. These men threw stones at Paul to kill him. They dragged him out of the city, thinking he was dead.

But when the believers gathered around Paul, he got right up and walked back into the city. God healed him! And Paul was strong enough to walk with Barnabas to another city the next day. The believers in Lystra saw God's power and trusted Him.

Paul and Barnabas made sure that each new church had leaders, called elders. They encouraged the believers to keep trusting God because "through many tribulations we must enter the kingdom of God" (Acts 14:22b). All believers will go through hard times in this world, but in Jesus' kingdom, everything will be good and new again!

. . . .

What good things did God do through Paul and Barnabas?

Big Meeting in Jerusalem
Acts 15

For the whole law is fulfilled in one word: "You shall love your neighbor as yourself."
GALATIANS 5:14

Has anyone ever told you a lie? Some men from Jerusalem were telling lies to the Gentile believers. They said that believing in Jesus wasn't enough to be part of God's family. They said everyone must follow all the Jewish laws and customs if they *really* wanted to be rescued.

Their lies made Paul and Barnabas angry. Paul and Barnabas knew the truth: No one can follow the rules by themselves because the rules are really about *love*. All people are broken. On our own, we can't truly love and do good as God created us to do. We all need God's Spirit to give us new hearts. Only then can we love as we were created to do.

Paul and Barnabas walked to Jerusalem to talk with Jesus' close friends, the apostles. They told the apostles about the wonderful things God was doing. He was rescuing both Jews *and* Gentiles.

During the meeting, Peter stood up and reminded everyone about the Gentile named Cornelius. Do you remember that story? Cornelius and everyone in his house believed that Jesus was the Rescuer, and God's Spirit came to be with them. Peter reminded them that no one—not even the Jews—was able to follow the law perfectly. And he said, "But we believe that we will be saved through the grace of the Lord Jesus, just as they will" (Acts 15:11).

Peter, James, and the other apostles knew that people were rescued by *Jesus*, not by trying to follow the rules. They wrote a letter to all the churches and sent it with Paul and Barnabas. The letter said that out of hundreds of laws, only a few still needed to be followed. Those few laws would show the Gentiles how to love God, love others, and love all creation. The letter also called the new believers brothers and sisters, which made the Gentile believers so happy! Because of Jesus, they were now part of God's family! They came close to God their Father and to each other.

. . . .

Peter said we are all saved by grace, a gift we can't earn or deserve. How would you describe grace?

Freedom in Galatia
Galatians

*If you are led by the Spirit, you are not under the law.... But the fruit of
the Spirit is love, joy, peace, patience, kindness, goodness, faithfulness,
gentleness, self-control; against such things there is no law.*
GALATIANS 5:18, 22–23

Paul and Barnabas traveled through an area called Galatia as they spoke to people about Jesus. Some of the people in Galatia had been pagans. Pagans did not worship the one true God. Often they worshipped pretend gods that they imagined had powers over nature. They wanted to know how to make it rain or how to grow plenty of food to eat.

But Paul taught the Galatians about freedom—freedom from the fear of pretend gods and also from laws that would not bring them closer to the one true God.

Some people said Gentiles must follow God's rules the way the Jews did if they wanted to be in God's kingdom. Other people said laws didn't matter anymore because of Jesus. But both of these ideas were wrong.

Many people had forgotten *why* God gave us rules and commands. Rules help us see evil and how we hurt others. Rules help us see good and how we can help others. Importantly, rules also help us see our need to be rescued. We can't always do good or love perfectly by ourselves—no one obeys the rules all the time.

But Jesus has a plan to help us. Paul wrote, "Christ redeemed us from the curse of the law by becoming a curse for us … so that in Christ Jesus the blessing of Abraham might come to the Gentiles, so that we might receive the promised Spirit through faith" (Galatians 3:13–14).

Jesus came to rescue all of us, both Jews and Gentiles. He came to bless all the families of the earth—just as God promised Abraham long ago. Jesus came to fulfill that promise and make everything new and good. He came to bring us close to Himself and to each other again. God's Spirit helps us love!

Paul taught the Galatians that real freedom is being able to do what we were created to do: love God, love others, and love all creation.

. . . .

How would you describe freedom? How does Jesus help us to be free?

Lydia by the River
Acts 16

For in one Spirit we were all baptized into one body—Jews or Greeks,
slaves or free—and all were made to drink of one Spirit.
1 CORINTHIANS 12:13

Paul decided to take his friend Silas on a new journey to tell people about Jesus. First they went back to places Paul had already been to encourage believers. They shared the good news that people are rescued by Jesus, not by trying to follow the law. And God's Spirit helped more people follow Jesus every day.

Paul wanted to go to a new place called Asia. But God's Spirit said, "Not yet." So they kept walking. Paul thought it would be good to go to a place called Mysia (MISH-ee-uh). But the Spirit of Jesus said, "Not yet." So they kept walking. Then one night, Paul had a vision: a man held out his hands and said, "Come to Macedonia and help us." So that's what Paul, Silas, and other friends did.

They sailed to Macedonia and stopped at a city called Philippi. They stayed there, searching for the man from the vision. But they didn't find him. There wasn't even a Jewish synagogue in Philippi.

One Sabbath, Paul and Silas went outside the city. They had heard that Jewish people met by the river to pray. They found people there—but they were all women!

Paul knew that Jesus came to rescue women too. Paul told them how Jesus, the true Son of God, came to rescue everyone who believes. Jesus came to wash away our sin and bring us close to God and to each other again.

A woman named Lydia heard Paul, and she believed! She was baptized, and her whole household believed, and they were baptized too. Lydia made a lot of money by selling expensive purple cloth. She knew Paul and his friends needed a place to stay. She invited everyone to stay at her house, and they did.

Through Paul, God rescued a woman named Lydia. Some people didn't think women were important, but Paul knew the truth. Jesus loves all people and rescues all who believe.

. . . .

Can you remember the very first time you heard about Jesus? What do you remember about that?

Singing in Prison
Acts 16

And we know that for those who love God all things work together for good, for those who are called according to his purpose.
ROMANS 8:28

Paul and Silas walked to the river in Philippi to teach the believers there. A slave girl saw them. She had an evil spirit, called a demon, inside her that claimed to tell the future. Many people came to listen to the demon, and they paid money to the girl's owners. The girl's owners were very proud of her and all the money.

But when the slave girl saw Paul and Silas, she started calling out that they were servants of the Most High God who would show the way of salvation. Her words confused people, and she kept shouting her message over and over, for many days.

Paul wanted that demon to come out. He said to the evil spirit, "I command you in the name of Jesus Christ to come out of her" (Acts 16:18). And the demon left right away!

But the girl's owners were very upset. They didn't care about her—they cared only about their money. They shouted lies about Paul and Silas, stirring up the crowds. Paul and Silas were arrested and beaten. Then they were chained inside a dark prison.

Around midnight, Paul and Silas were praying and singing songs to God. Suddenly a big earthquake shook the floor. The prison doors opened, and everyone's chains fell off! The jailer woke up and saw the open doors. He knew that he could be punished, even killed, for letting the prisoners escape. But Paul shouted, "We're all here!"

The jailer couldn't believe it! He rushed in and fell down before Paul and Silas. The jailer knew their God was special—not only did God help them sing in prison, He helped them *escape* from prison! The jailer asked, "Sirs, what must I do to be saved?" Paul and Silas answered, "Believe in the Lord Jesus, and you will be saved" (verses 30–31). The jailer invited them to his home. Everyone in his house heard the good news about Jesus. His whole family believed, and they were all baptized!

The next morning, the city leaders let Paul and Silas go free. The two disciples went to visit Lydia and the other believers. Then they left Philippi.

. . . .

How did God turn something sad into something very good?

Travels among the Greeks
Acts 17–18

He has delivered us from the domain of darkness and transferred us to the kingdom of his beloved Son, in whom we have redemption, the forgiveness of sins.
COLOSSIANS 1:13–14

After they left Philippi, Paul and Silas traveled to Thessalonica (THESS-uh-luh-NYE-kuh). Paul went to the Jewish synagogue and told people that Jesus was the Messiah. Some of the Jews believed, and many Gentiles and important Greek women believed too. But some Jewish men who didn't believe in Jesus were angry and stirred up the crowds. Paul and Silas had to sneak out of Thessalonica at night.

They went to a new town and spoke in the synagogue there too. Again, many Jews heard the good news and believed. But the angry Jews from Thessalonica followed Paul and Silas to this new town and stirred up the crowds there. This time the believers sent Paul off by himself, and he sailed across the sea to another city called Athens.

Athens was an important Greek city full of statues and buildings built for pretend gods. Paul wanted the people of Athens to know the one true God. He told many people about the true God who made the whole world. He is the God who gives life to everything, and He wants us to be close to Him. Paul told them, "He is actually not far from each one of us, for 'In him we live and move and have our being'" (Acts 17:27b–28a). Some of the people in Athens believed.

After Paul left Athens, he went to another city called Corinth. He entered the synagogue and told people about the Messiah. Crispus, the leader of the synagogue, believed that Jesus was the Messiah. Many other Corinthians believed too, and they were baptized.

Paul met a Jewish couple, Aquila and Priscilla, and they became friends. This couple earned money by making tents, just as Paul did. Together they taught people in Corinth about Jesus. And God encouraged Paul in a vision. God said, "Don't be afraid. Keep speaking, for I am with you, and no one will hurt you. Many of My people are in this city." So Paul stayed in Corinth for a long time, telling people about the Rescuer.

. . . .

Can you think of someone who needs to hear about Jesus, our Rescuer? How could you tell that person about Jesus?

Paul and the Sorcerers' Scrolls
Acts 19

Put on the whole armor of God, that you may be able to stand against the schemes of the devil. For we do not wrestle against flesh and blood, but against the rulers, against the authorities, against the cosmic powers over this present darkness.
EPHESIANS 6:11–12a

Paul went to a city called Ephesus. He met believers who knew they needed the Messiah, but they didn't know *Jesus* was the Messiah. When Paul taught them, they believed and were baptized. Then Paul laid his hands on them, and God's Spirit came to them.

Paul stayed in Ephesus for two years, telling people about Jesus and God's kingdom. God's Spirit did unusual miracles through Paul. Someone could even take a handkerchief or an apron that had touched Paul and touch a sick person with the cloth, and he or she would be healed!

Ephesus was a city filled with beliefs in magical powers. At this time other Jews were claiming to cast out evil spirits. They made a big show of this power. A Jewish priest named Sceva (SKEE-vah) had seven sons who claimed to cast out demons. They wanted to use Jesus' power, but they weren't close to Jesus like Paul was. So when the sons said to a demon, "I command you by the Jesus that Paul preaches," the demon didn't listen at all. The evil spirit answered, "Jesus I know, and Paul I recognize, but who are you?" (Acts 19:15). And then the demon-possessed man beat all seven sons, and they ran away naked and hurt.

People saw the good and true things God's Spirit was doing through Paul. They stopped using magic and turned to the living God. They burned their magic books and scrolls. The books cost *so* much money—fifty thousand pieces of silver! But people knew being good friends with God and each other was much better than using magic or worshipping pretend gods.

However, not everyone agreed. A man named Demetrius (duh-MEE-tree-us) sold silver idols of pretend gods. When people started believing in the one true God, they stopped buying his idols. Demetrius was angry and stirred up the crowds. Paul wanted to talk to the angry people, but it wasn't safe. Finally, one of the town leaders calmed everyone down.

. . . .

How can believing in pretend gods hurt people?

One Big Body
1 Corinthians

Now you are the body of Christ and individually members of it.
1 CORINTHIANS 12:27

While Paul was living in the city of Ephesus, he still thought about the churches in other places. God's Spirit helped Paul love the believers in *all* the cities. Paul wrote letters to them. His letter to the church in Corinth talked about "the body of Christ."

You probably know that there are many different parts that make up your body. We have eyes that see, ears that hear, and noses that smell. All our body parts work together to help us live well. If we didn't have feet, we'd have trouble walking. If we didn't have tongues, we'd have trouble talking. Every part matters.

In the same way, each person who believes in Jesus matters. Jesus helps us work together with His Spirit to love God and love others and make things good and new again. When we follow Jesus and trust Him, He makes us part of what He's doing everywhere and for everyone—part of His body of believers. Paul wrote, "For in one Spirit we were all baptized into one body—Jews or Greeks, slaves or free" (1 Corinthians 12:13a).

In the part of the world where Paul lived, people thought feet were *very* embarrassing and "unclean." No one showed others the bottoms of their feet unless they were trying to be mean. If people could choose to be part of Jesus' body, no one would choose to be a foot!

But Paul taught the Corinthians that every part of Jesus' body of believers was important. No one was worth more or less than another. And no part should be working against another part. Instead, God wants us to have "no division in the body, but that the members may have the same care for one another. If one member suffers, all suffer together; if one member is honored, all rejoice together" (verses 25–26).

In God's church, or His body of believers, we all need each other. Each person matters, even the person who seems unimportant or different or embarrassing. God's Spirit brings us together and helps us love each other. We all have a place in His good kingdom.

You matter to God, and He loves you.

. . . .

What do you think about the idea that the church is like a body? How does it help you to know that every person matters to God?

MAP

3

The Good News Spreads

As Paul and other friends of Jesus told everyone the good news about the Rescuer, many more people believed. These people became close to God and to each other. Some of them were healed, some of them saw God's power, and all of them felt God's love. And as they came to know God and His story better, they wanted to tell others that story too. They wanted others to know that Jesus, the Rescuer, was making everything good and new again. The good news about Jesus spread from city to city and nation to nation. And it is still spreading today! Look on the map and see if you can find places you know where people have heard about Jesus. Where are some places you would like to go? Who would you like to tell about Jesus?

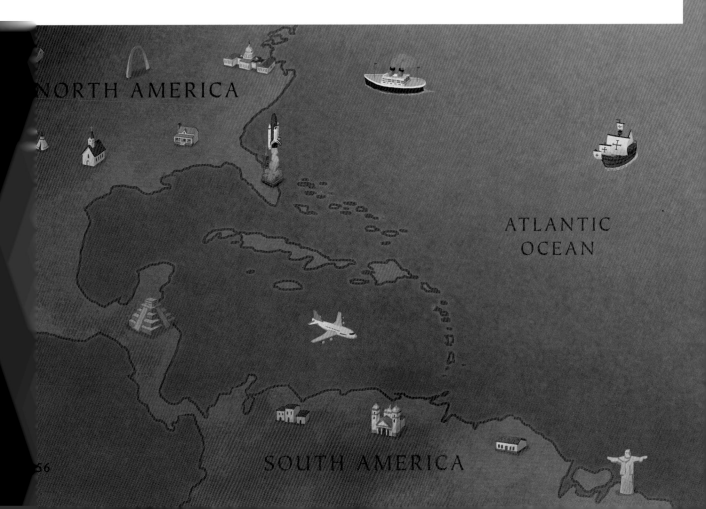

NORTH AMERICA

ATLANTIC OCEAN

SOUTH AMERICA

EUROPE

ASIA

AFRICA

Sleepy Eutychus
Acts 20–21

*For to me to live is Christ, and to die is gain.… My desire is to
depart and be with Christ, for that is far better.*
PHILIPPIANS 1:21, 23b

When Paul went to a city called Troas, he couldn't stay long. On his last day there, Paul was talking with a large group of believers in an upper room. He kept talking very late into the night because he had to leave the next day. As Paul taught, a young man named Eutychus (YOO-ti-kus) was listening—or trying to. He was sitting at the window opening, high up on the third story. But he sank into a deep sleep. As his body slumped, he fell out of the window and died.

But Paul went down to Eutychus and lifted him up. Then Paul told people, "Don't be afraid; he's not dead." Eutychus had come back to life!

Paul ate with his friends and kept talking until the sun came up, and then he left Troas. Paul and some friends set sail. Paul was in a hurry to be in Jerusalem to celebrate the holiday called Pentecost.

On the way to Jerusalem, the ship stopped at different cities. Paul asked his close friends from Ephesus to come visit him. Paul told his friends, "I have done the work God gave me to do. I have told both Jews and Greeks about Jesus and His kingdom. And now I'm going to Jerusalem. God's Spirit has told me I will be put in prison. I will suffer. You will not see my face again. But remember God's grace and how He has rescued you."

Paul prayed with his friends, and everyone cried. Then Paul left. He stopped at another city and met with friends there. A prophet named Agabus (AG-uh-bus) came to visit Paul. He took Paul's belt and tied up his own hands and feet. Then he said, "God's Spirit says, 'This is how the Jews at Jerusalem will tie you up and give you to the Gentiles.'"

Paul's friends begged him not to go, but he knew what God wanted him to do. He was ready. Ever since Paul met Jesus, everything had changed. Paul saw how beautiful and powerful Jesus, the Rescuer, is—and he wanted everyone else to see His beauty and power! Paul knew that when he left this broken world, he would be glad to be with Jesus forever.

. . . .

What was going to happen when Paul went to Jerusalem? Why didn't Paul run away?

Everyone Needs Jesus
Romans

For all have sinned and fall short of the glory of God, and are justified by his grace as a gift, through the redemption that is in Christ Jesus.
ROMANS 3:23–24

Before Paul went to Jerusalem, he wrote a letter to the believers in Rome—the capital city of the Roman Empire. He wanted them to know about sin and God's grace. Many people, especially the Jews, thought that sin was just about breaking one of God's rules. But Paul knew that God's rules were actually about *love*. Sinning means not loving God, people, or creation. It means knowing what being loving is yet choosing to do something else.

People were made to love and be loved. Long ago, God created the world and the first people. God loved His people. But the people believed Satan's lies instead of their good Creator's truth. They disobeyed God, and their friendship with Him and with each other was broken. *Everything* was broken.

Paul reminded the Romans that one day all creation would be set free and people could live again as children of God. Ever since sin had entered the world, creation had been broken and hurting. But one day God will bring new life!

Sin is much worse than breaking a law—it's breaking our friendship with God, others, and all creation. And Paul reminded the Romans that *everyone* sins: "All have sinned and fall short of the glory of God" (Romans 3:23). But the good news is that everyone can receive the gift of God's grace. Everyone can be forgiven and made new.

No one can truly love in the perfect way God created. That's why Jesus came. He died in our place for our sin, and then He came back to life to give *us* new life! Jesus changes our hearts so that we can truly love Him and each other. He brings us close to Himself through the gift of grace—He knows we can't come close on our own.

Paul wrote, "But God shows his love for us in that while we were still sinners, Christ died for us" (5:8). God loves us so much! He is rescuing us and making all things new. He is bringing His good kingdom to earth, and He wants us to be part of it.

. . . .

What does it mean to sin? Why does everyone need Jesus to rescue them?

No More Walls
Acts 21

There is neither Jew nor Greek, there is neither slave nor free,
there is no male and female, for you are all one in Christ Jesus.
GALATIANS 3:28

When Paul arrived in Jerusalem, he met with Jesus' close friends, the apostles. Paul told them how God had rescued people—even the Gentiles! The apostles were very happy and praised God. But there was a problem: Many Jews had believed in Jesus, but they still thought *everyone* must follow the law the same way they did. These Jews were angry with Paul—they thought he was telling the Gentiles that the law didn't matter.

Paul was actually teaching that *no one* could follow the law perfectly. The law shows us how to love, but all people are broken. The angry Jews didn't understand Paul or his message.

But James and the elders had an idea. Paul could show the Jews that he still loved the law. Paul and four other men who had made a promise to God could go to the Temple. At the Temple they would give an offering and clean themselves as the law required.

When Paul went to the Temple, he passed several walls. One wall separated the outer court from the Court of Women. Gentiles could not pass this wall. Signs stated, "Any foreigners who pass this point will be responsible for their own deaths." Then Paul passed a wall that Jewish women could not pass. Only Jewish men could enter the Court of Israel.

A group of Jews from Asia saw Paul and stirred up the crowds. They shouted lies, saying Paul had allowed "unclean" Gentiles into their holy Temple. They dragged Paul out of the Temple and beat him. The whole city was in an uproar. Then Roman soldiers came and carried Paul away.

The Temple had many walls that separated people from God and each other. The walls separated Gentiles from Jews. They also separated men from women. But Paul knew that God wanted all people to come close to Him and to each other.

. . . .

How can hearing about Jesus bring people together?

Paul Tells His Story
Acts 22–23

But avoid foolish controversies, genealogies, dissensions, and quarrels
about the law, for they are unprofitable and worthless.
TITUS 3:9

It was a dangerous time in Jerusalem. The Roman soldiers tried to get Paul away from an angry mob. But Paul wanted to speak. When he spoke to the crowd in their own Hebrew language, a hush fell over the people.

Paul told everyone his story. He was Jewish, born in a foreign city. But he had lived in Jerusalem, learning from a famous Jewish teacher named Gamaliel. Paul loved the law. He became a Pharisee, a strict teacher of the law. He tried to get rid of anyone who believed that Jesus was the Messiah. Paul had wanted everyone who followed the Way to be put in prison or even killed. But when he met Jesus on the road to Damascus, everything changed. God sent Paul to both the Jews and the Gentiles. He told everyone that Jesus the Messiah came to rescue us and make all things new.

When Paul said that Jesus came for the Gentiles too, the angry crowd began shouting. They took off their cloaks and made a cloud of dust. A Roman official ordered Paul inside. He planned to whip Paul to find out why the people were so angry.

But when the soldiers tied Paul up, he asked, "Does the law say you can whip a Roman citizen without a trial?"

The centurion standing by went and told the Roman official that Paul was a citizen. The soldiers were afraid and left. But the next day, the Roman leader took Paul to a meeting of Jewish religious leaders. He wanted to know what they thought about Paul.

Paul spoke to the leaders: "Brothers, I am a Pharisee, from a family of Pharisees. I'm here because of my hope that God will bring life out of death."

Paul's words caused a fight among the religious leaders. Some believed that God would bring new life out of death, while others did not. The leaders began shouting and became violent. The Roman soldiers rescued Paul again, afraid that he would be torn to pieces.

. . . .

Why do you think these people were so angry about what Paul was saying?

Paul Speaks in Prison
Acts 23–26

*"You will be my witnesses in Jerusalem and in all Judea and Samaria,
and to the end of the earth."*
ACTS 1:8b

So many people were angry with Paul. But one night Jesus said to him, "Take courage. Just as you have told people about Me in Jerusalem, you will tell about Me in Rome."

The next day, some angry Jews made a plan. More than forty men promised not to eat or drink anything until Paul was dead. But Paul's nephew heard about their plan and told Paul. Paul told his guards, and the Roman leaders gathered two hundred soldiers, seventy horsemen, and two hundred men with spears to take Paul away at night. It was dangerous to travel in the dark, but the soldiers took Paul to a city called Caesarea (sess-uh-REE-uh) to keep him safe. There Paul would be judged by Felix the governor.

Five days later, the Jewish leaders traveled to Caesarea. They said Paul caused riots and broke their laws. They said Paul should be killed. But Paul said he was not guilty. He said, "I follow the Way. I worship the God of our fathers, and I believe everything written in the Law and Prophets. My hope is in God, who will bring life out of death."

Felix the governor knew about both Paul and the Way. But he waited to make a decision and kept Paul in prison. Felix told the soldiers to be kind to Paul. Paul's friends were allowed to bring him food and other things he needed.

Paul was a prisoner in that city for more than two years. He spoke to Roman leaders, telling them how Jesus changed his life and was making all things new. Paul said, "The prophets and Moses said that Christ must suffer. But 'by being the first to rise from the dead, he would proclaim light both to our people and to the Gentiles'" (Acts 26:23).

Finally, Paul said that he needed to tell Caesar, the leader of the Roman Empire, that he was not guilty. The other Roman leaders saw that Paul was speaking true words. But because Paul asked to see Caesar, they sent Paul to Rome.

. . . .

Who did Paul tell about Jesus? Paul kept talking about Jesus, even in prison. How can you show people the hope and love of Jesus—no matter where you go?

Letters of Love
1 Corinthians, Colossians, 1 and 2 John

Beloved, let us love one another, for love is from God, and whoever loves has been born of God and knows God. Anyone who does not love does not know God, because God is love.
1 JOHN 4:7–8

While Paul was in prison, he had plenty of time to write letters to the churches. Other apostles wrote letters too. One thing they all wrote about was love. We were made to love and be loved. Love is who God is, and love is what He created us to enjoy.

Paul wrote to followers of Jesus in the city of Colossae (coh-LOSS-ay). They were struggling in their faith because of false teachings. Colossians made a beautiful dark red cloth in their city. Imagine important people wearing red sashes or robes. The dark red stood out against the brown and green of the land. But Paul wanted people to stand out in a different way. He wrote, "Put on then, as God's chosen ones, holy and beloved, compassionate hearts, kindness, humility, meekness, and patience.... And above all these put on love, which binds everything together in perfect harmony" (Colossians 3:12, 14).

Paul knew that Jesus changes people's hearts and helps them love. Just as people might put on a red robe or scarf, Paul wanted believers to choose to put on love so everyone could see it.

Another letter encouraged believers to love not just with words but "in deed and in truth" (1 John 3:18b). But what does it mean to love?

Paul wrote about love to the believers in Corinth: "Love is patient and kind; love does not envy or boast; it is not arrogant or rude. It does not insist on its own way; it is not irritable or resentful; it does not rejoice at wrongdoing, but rejoices with the truth" (1 Corinthians 13:4–6).

Love means meeting the needs of another, even at great cost to yourself. Love is wanting good for someone and then *doing* that good, even if it's hard to do.

Love is beautiful. One day we will see God and His love face to face! He will help us love Him, love others, and love all creation. Everything will be good and new again.

. . . .

Can you think of someone who loves you? How do you know that person loves you?

Stormy Seas and Shipwrecks
Acts 27

For the sake of Christ, then, I am content with weaknesses, insults, hardships,
persecutions, and calamities. For when I am weak, then I am strong.
2 CORINTHIANS 12:10

While Paul was in prison, God spoke to him in a vision. God told Paul that he would share the truth about Jesus' rescue not only in Jerusalem but also in Rome. And now, since Paul had asked to see Caesar, it was time to get on a ship. Roman soldiers guarded Paul and other prisoners. Julius, the Roman centurion in charge, was kind to Paul. When the ship stopped, Julius let Paul visit his friends in those cities.

But the wind blew against the ship. The time of year for big, dangerous storms came. Paul warned the soldiers not to keep sailing. But the soldiers didn't listen.

Then a fierce wind came. It pushed the ship farther and farther out to sea. The ship climbed high up one wave, then came crashing back down, over and over. Everyone was afraid the ship would sink. The sailors began throwing heavy things into the sea.

For many days all was dark. They didn't see the sun or the stars. No one could eat— they were too seasick. Everyone gave up hope. They all thought they would die.

Finally, God spoke to Paul in a vision. God said, "Do not be afraid, Paul; you must stand before Caesar. And behold, God has granted you all those who sail with you" (Acts 27:24). Paul told everyone, "You should have listened to me and not set sail. But now, take heart, because God has told me that no one will die. We will only lose the ship. I have faith in God that it will happen exactly as He said. The ship will run aground on an island."

And that's just what happened.

After fourteen days, the ship reached land. Paul encouraged everyone to eat and told them, "Not a hair is to perish from the head of any of you" (verse 34b). Paul took bread, gave thanks to God, broke it, and began to eat. And everyone else ate too. Then they sailed the ship straight into the nearest land, and the ship struck a reef and broke apart.

When the ship broke, they all jumped into the sea—soldiers, sailors, and prisoners. Then everyone swam safely to the island, just as God had promised Paul.

. . . .

How did God show His goodness and power to everyone on the ship?

Wonders on Malta
Acts 28

For I am sure that neither death nor life, nor angels nor rulers, nor things present nor things to come, nor powers, nor height nor depth, nor anything else in all creation, will be able to separate us from the love of God in Christ Jesus our Lord.
ROMANS 8:38–39

On the island of Malta, Paul and the other shipwreck survivors met kind people. It was raining and cold, so the native people built a fire for them. Paul was gathering sticks for the fire when a snake bit him. The native people saw the viper on his hand and said, "He must be a bad man. He escaped the sea, but our goddess Justice won't let him live."

But Paul shook the snake off into the fire. They watched Paul and waited for something terrible to happen—they thought he would swell up or fall down dead. But nothing happened! When they saw that Paul was saved again, they thought he must be a god.

Publius, the leader of the island, invited everyone from the ship to stay with him. They stayed for three days. While Paul was there, he heard that Publius's father was very sick. Paul laid his hands on the sick man and prayed, and the man was healed! All the islanders heard what had happened. They brought everyone who was sick, and God healed them all. And the people of Malta learned about the one true God!

After three months, Paul and the others found another ship and left the island. The native people gave them everything they needed for the trip to Rome.

In Rome the believers traveled a long way to meet Paul. He thanked God for them. He was still a prisoner, but he could stay in his own house with a guard.

A few days later, Paul met some Jewish leaders. He told them that Jesus was the promised Messiah. Some believed, but others did not. Paul reminded them that the prophet Isaiah had foretold that some wouldn't believe. Paul said, "Therefore let it be known to you that this salvation of God has been sent to the Gentiles; they will listen" (Acts 28:28).

Paul stayed in Rome for two more years. Many people came to visit him. He told all of them about Jesus and His work to make all things new.

- -

How did the people of Malta hear about the one true God and believe? What are your favorite stories about the power of God?

Onesimus Set Free
Philemon

I appeal to you for my child, Onesimus, whose father I became in my imprisonment … that you might have him back forever, no longer as a bondservant but more than a bondservant, as a beloved brother.
PHILEMON 10, 15b–16a

While Paul was in prison, he met a slave named Onesimus (oh-NESS-i-muss). Slaves were workers owned by other people. A slave master paid money to buy a person to work without pay, and then the slave had to do whatever the master wanted. Slave masters could be very mean to their slaves and never get in trouble.

Onesimus didn't want to be a slave anymore. He ran away. But he was scared that someone would find out. Some runaway slaves were punished terribly.

When Onesimus met Paul, many things changed. Paul told Onesimus about the one true God, the Rescuer who came to make all things new. Onesimus believed! He was set free from sin and death. He became part of God's family. Onesimus was given new life.

But he was still a runaway slave. When Onesimus told Paul about his master, Philemon (fye-LEE-mun), Paul knew what to do. He had already told Philemon about Jesus, and Philemon had believed. God had rescued Philemon too, bringing him close to God and to other people. God was helping Philemon love. Philemon even invited the other believers to his big house so they could meet together.

Paul wrote to Philemon. He wanted Philemon to see Onesimus as a brother, not as a runaway slave. He wanted Philemon to love Onesimus, just as Philemon loved other believers. Paul knew that slaves were expensive. Philemon would lose a lot of money if he set Onesimus free. Paul promised to pay Philemon that money.

Paul wanted the broken friendship between Onesimus and Philemon to be healed. And he wanted Philemon to set Onesimus free. Paul wrote, "Confident of your obedience, I write to you, knowing that you will do even more than I say" (verse 21).

. . . .

What is wrong about a person owning another person? How did Jesus change the lives of Onesimus and Philemon?

New Heaven and Earth
Revelation

Then I saw a new heaven and a new earth, for the first heaven and the first earth had passed away, and the sea was no more.... And he who was seated on the throne said, "Behold, I am making all things new."
REVELATION 21:1, 5a

John was a close friend of Jesus, like Paul and Peter. For a while John was exiled to the island of Patmos—sent there by people who treated Jesus' friends badly. God gave John a vision. John saw Jesus again! Jesus wore a long robe with a golden sash. His hair was white like snow, and His eyes were like fire. His feet were like shining bronze, and His voice was like roaring water. Jesus' face was as bright as the sun. And John fell down at His feet.

But Jesus put His right hand on John and said, "Fear not, I am the first and the last, and the living one. I died, and behold I am alive forevermore, and I have the keys of Death and Hades" (Revelation 1:17b–18). And Jesus told John to write down everything he saw.

After Jesus gave John seven messages for seven different churches in Asia, John saw many things. He saw the brokenness of people and the world, and he saw the glory of God. But do you know one of the best things John saw?

John saw a beautiful city come down out of heaven. It was God's city. And a loud voice said, "Behold, the dwelling place of God is with man. He will dwell with them, and they will be his people, and God himself will be with them as their God" (21:3).

One day people will be *with God*! The voice continued, "He will wipe away every tear from their eyes, and death shall be no more, neither shall there be mourning, nor crying, nor pain anymore, for the former things have passed away" (verse 4).

God will make everything good and new again. No one will get hurt or cry. No one will get sick or die. All these promises will come true through *grace*. Jesus will make all things new just because He loves us, not because we are good enough. Jesus rescues all who realize their need for Him—every person who believes. He invites us into His new kingdom. And we can invite others too!

. . . .

What things will be different when God makes all things new? Who would you like to see in God's city?

Oh sing to the Lord a new song,
    for he has done marvelous things!
His right hand and his holy arm
    have worked salvation for him.
The Lord has made known his salvation;
    he has revealed his righteousness in the sight
    of the nations.
He has remembered his steadfast love and faithfulness
    to the house of Israel.
All the ends of the earth have seen
    the salvation of our God.

Make a joyful noise to the Lord, all the earth;
    break forth into joyous song and sing praises!
Sing praises to the Lord with the lyre,
    with the lyre and the sound of melody!
With trumpets and the sound of the horn
    make a joyful noise before the King, the Lord!

Let the sea roar, and all that fills it;
    the world and those who dwell in it!
Let the rivers clap their hands;
    let the hills sing for joy together
before the Lord, for he comes
    to judge the earth.
He will judge the world with righteousness,
    and the peoples with equity.

PSALM 98

ACKNOWLEDGMENTS

A new children's book, like a new birth, involves months and months of planning, working, growing, and consulting with experts. When the book is finally in your hands, it's hard not to tear up in awe and gratitude. As with the previous books in this series, I remain incredibly thankful for the contributing experts. Laura Derico, the editor, always makes things better. Ian Dale, the illustrator, continues to amaze me with the beautifully poignant images he dreams up and brings to life. My ever-patient and supportive husband, Matt Richie, faithfully juggles a few more items in order to give me the needed time to write. And all four of our beautiful children continue to grow, ask questions, listen to stories, and provide both inspiration and insight. The stories I write are always addressed first to them, and then our family has the joy of watching the books spread across the world. In fact, *The Advent Storybook* is now available in both Korean and Slovak!

The months and years during which this book grew and took shape have not been easy. The COVID-19 pandemic has harmed or taken so many lives, and many people are even now exhausted, including my fellow health care workers. Other challenges buffeted simultaneously, and I have had some very dark days. But God has remained constant and faithful, and He often placed just the right person in my life at the right time. One such person is my friend Chriss Zielke, whose encouragement and generosity I will never forget.

Unlike the first two storybooks in this series, *The Go-and-Tell Storybook* isn't associated with a holiday. Both the publisher and I expressed concern that families might not be as interested as a result, but I felt strongly that God wanted me to continue the Story. I hope that families will choose a different month that works for them and read through these thirty stories, learning how the mission of Jesus didn't end with His ascension but continued through His Spirit empowering His friends.

Through many dark, heart-wrenching days, I have continued to hold on to the hope that Jesus, our Rescuer, is making all things good and new. Evil, suffering, and death will not last, because the powerful and good Son of God died and rose again to bring us back to Himself. Wholeness, true life, and beauty are the unfolding reality of all who believe in Jesus. We see glimmers even now, shining through the darkness, and we long for the day when faith becomes sight. May we join hands to hope and work in God's kingdom, where all things are new.

ABOUT THE CREATORS

Laura Richie is a wife, homeschooling mom, and registered nurse. A missionary kid for several years, Laura confesses she didn't truly understand her need to be rescued until later in life. Now she delights in sharing the beauty and grace of her Rescuer. Laura lives in Oklahoma with her husband and four children.

Ian Dale is an illustrator and designer who loves to invest in projects that share the hope and meaning that have transformed his life. He has created art for clients including World Vision, American Bible Society, Compassion International, and *The Bible App for Kids*, which has been downloaded in more than fifty languages. Ian lives in Southern California with his wife and two children. Visit him online at iandale.net.

Enjoy all the titles in the **Storybook Series!**